Precious Girl | Words From ₥ᵧ

John Gumbs

Printed in the United Kingdom
First Edition, December 2020
ISBN 978-1-8383775-0-2
John Gumbs

Cover Art & Book Layout Designer - Rotimi Skyers
Instagram: romeysky

CONTENT

PREFACE

My journey as a poet, started during the UK national Corona Virus lockdown in March 2020. The poems started, through a human need to remain productive and creative, whilst being quarantined for weeks.

I suddenly started to write small poems on my Instagram account - After never, ever seriously written any poetry before.

I instantly began to get very positive feedback from other poets and people in general. This led to me a month or so later performing some of my original poems on a stage in central London - headlining with another poet, who was also the show director. The audience enjoyed our performances - the feedback was extremely positive and heartfelt.

After months of continued positive comments and critiques of my poems, I decided I would produce a small collection of my work.

I'm a boxing trainer, from the world famous Miguel's Boxing Gym in Brixton, London. From boxing to poetry, is quite a contrast for me, but poetry, somehow, feels like a calling. Time and fate, will tell.

My first childhood memories, were as a baby, in my mother's arms. I remember been placed in my cot and staring at the clouds, through the bedroom window. Such vivid memories. My mother's love, I could feel, beaming from her eyes - before I had words to speak, I knew what love was. My parent's marriage dissolved while I was still very young and my father became a very loving single parent, of two small children - my younger sister and I. My mother was not physically close to me, for many years after the breakup, but I still felt that piercing love. I always knew she was and remains a precious, girl.

My inner worlds have always been coloured by that feminine, magical love. This collection of poems are just a small snapshot of my inner experiences, often sensed so differently, that I call them "worlds". Worlds of love philosophy and spirit - filtered through the art of poetry.

Precious Girl is a collection of short poems - my first ever book.

I hope readers get some value and possibly some enjoyment, from my inner worlds.

This book dedicated to true love.

1

OF THE HEART

As you come back to life
Precious girl
Embracing what is to be
Precious girl
Every fate
That comes to you
You will always
Master through
Protect your soul
Keep loving new
Precious girl

Master

There's no way
I couldn't love you
No way
There's no words
For your beauty
So I won't say
There's no measure for you
So compare
I won't do
There's no way
I couldn't love you
No way

Measure

You take my breath away
It's just what you do
Slowed till it's gone
If only you knew
Can't understand your magic
From another world
Passing through
You take my breath away
Every time I see you

Breath

I miss you
Like the heart
Misses the beat
I miss you
Like the Sun
Misses the heat
I miss you
Like the babe
Misses the breast
You're my best
From the heart
I miss you

Misses

Everytime
I think of you
I'm lost
Somewhere dark and cold
With a feeling
Like the frost
Learnt some magic now
I just speak your name
Then my way is lit
When
I'm lost
I think of you
Everytime

Everytime

Poisoned by beauty
Made ill by a perfect form
Hurt by a being so lovely
Ripped up by pure joy and then torn
Stabbed deep by an ecstatic creation
Brutally struck by a vision that's true
Poisoned by beauty
And died loving you

Poisoned

Say goodbye
You may never see them again
Give a smile
Be warm
Moments are golden
Speak love into ears
Delight the soul
Treasure her being
Keep precious dear
Act not in fear
Please swear
You may never see them again
Say goodbye

Goodbye

Not everyone will love you
Not everyone will care
Some will come
Just for a season
And run their fingers through your hair
Some will hurt you with mere words
But you're beautiful
Take care
Not everyone will love you
But love don't stop
Deep breath
Prepare

Hair

Deep in thought
Full of love
It's so in you
Deep in thought
Living dreams
From a world
The beautiful knew
Deep in thought
Here for a moment
Then you've gone
Like a kiss
Deep in thought
So very special
So deep in thought

Living

Did someone steal your world
Run off with all your dreams
Did someone remove your heart
Make you hurt yourself and scream
Did you forget as a fool
How lovingly dear you are
The most valuable gem
You're so precious to me you're a star
There's no other
Please be true
To you
Darling
Become
True
To you

Steal

There's a palace of gold
I built
Just for you
It's filled with treasures
I found in your mind
So many rooms
Each with views
Designed with love
Poured and glued
Just for you
I built
A palace of gold

Glued

Words can't say
How the clouds
Blow away
And the stars every night
Light the skies
How you move
On the ground
How your glow
Warms and sounds
Blow away
How clouds move
Words can't say

Ground

Sarah's eyes
As they view
They see all that you do
Then she smiles
Glowing brighter than the Sun
Sarah's eyes
Match her voice
Made in Heaven
God's special choice
She moves with love
This you can see
In Sarah's eyes

Sarah

I'll clothe you
In the colour of blue
And timeless gold
You won't get old
You'll discover
Your inner lover
In pink
Don't you think
In red
You'll be a danger
In white
A space ranger
Dressed sharp in black
Would you come back
Take my ring
Here's what I'll do
In the colour of blue
I'll clothe you

Clothe

Could you love an angel
Who had no wings
Or one who couldn't write
One who couldn't sing
Could you love an angel
Who had no hair
Who couldn't see
Came down from heaven bare
Would it matter
Do you think
All of that
If she loved you

Bare

One complete light
One wondrous view
One soul ever deep
One passion so true
One life living free
One gift from on high
One day of all days
One space where I fly
One love worth all effort
One love so brand new
One love at a time
One love only you
Only you

One

The good from goodbye
That Sun after rain
That torment and sorrow
That made love come again
Those blows so brutal
Saw a dream come true
Now the rain has stopped falling
Enjoy the Sun
It's for you

Torment

I believe in you
More than you believe in you
Is that love
I see your magic
More than anyone else
Ever could
Is that love
When you're down
I lift you up
In your thirst
I become a cup
Filled with you
And you drink
Is that love

Thirst

I'm so glad
For my dad
He gave me all
The love he had
I'm never sad
Too much joy
Love you dad

Gave

Electrified by you
Unshaken by fate
Love outside of love's normal
A truth written in slate
Prolific energies overwhelming
Only one was made of you
A quiet tree with roots eternal
I'm
Electrified by you

Electrified

I traversed a desert alone
I've been a king
I've been a fisherman
I've had nothing
I've been enlightened
I've been a slave
I've been a monk
I've misbehaved
I've been a fool
I've left fools talking
But love with you
I've been everything

Talking

Write me a poem
That will make me change
One that touches my soul
I beg please create from your heart once again
Only use precious words
That you've kissed and you've blessed
Write me a poem
Make me change darling
I'm sorry
I love
You
Less

Poem

Mona Lisa, staying home
Quarantined, but not in Rome
Her fate is always unbeknown
Mona Lisa, all alone

Mona

I think of you
More than you
Think of me
And you think of me
All the time
It's not possible
But still incredible
Mysteries exist
Until
The
End
Of
Time

Mysteries

I don't dream your dreams
I don't walk in your shoes
I don't think your thoughts
Or see this world just like you
I can't imagine your journey
And what fate has put you through
But I'll listen
And be present
That's all I can do

Present

2

LONDON

In my city
Tailored to look pretty
Pedestrians avoid the cars
People hustle
Interests tussle
Children never knowing stars
It may look easy
Stomachs queasy
London streets ain't paved with gold
Sparks still bright
Roam late at night
Grasping memories, before their cold

Sparks

She
Who is tired of London
Is probably
Very tired
London does that
To all

She

Another full Moon
Over Brixton
One more day has spun away
Can't see the stars
Only streetlights
And angelic souls
That guide my way

Brixton

She never knew
The beauty she had
All her life
Was confusion and pain
Family disowned her
Strange people gave her orders
Professionals discussed her brain
Living in various cities
That never showed any pity
She never knew
How I loved her
She never knew
How she shone
She never knew
The beauty she had

Disowned

Locked down by Corona
With time to think
What London and I have gone through
What did we both value
How did we differ
What made us happy
What made us blue

I'll walk by the Thames
And think of friends
Knowing those people
Came down from above
Please don't for a second
Not even a tick
Neglect souls, sent to you to love

Thames

I went to school
And met a friend
He shone like a star
My father said
He lived a life
That made me proud
I say it loud
I had a friend

Proud

She wore a silver jacket
Her blonde hair caught with the wind
Rushing through city traffic
A busy schedule she had just trimmed
Her smile was always welcoming
Helpfulness was her main grace
When evening came she rested
Angels hovering over that space

Jacket

Lockdown is coming
Everyone prepare
No need to worry
Even though the media scare
Lockdown is coming
Have you PPE and toilet roll
No need to worry
Boris and Trump
Are in control

Lockdown

It's a hot summer's day
The soul of Brixton is sound
In between the ropes
In the ring
Champions everywhere found
People from every world
Drawn by an angel up high
Burpees, tuck jumps, sit-ups
Battle ropes made one cry
From voices highly regarded
That gym has helped so many lives
Miguel's gym
Always and forever
Feel the love
And unity
Punching together
The good survive

Miguel's

Another sunny day
Lorries always in view
Outside playing football
Police cars shooting through
Making noise on the bus
Playing music way too loud
Buying clothes in the West End
Walking at speed
With the crowd
Everyone's always happy
Except that nutter
Making a name
Back to school again on Monday
London's always the same

Sunny

In my school
We were taught to read
In a corner huddled
Teachers tried but
Many minds remained muddled
In my school
Big boys ruled but
Pretty girls made them fool
In my school
We learnt chemistry in the loft
Electrons move said angry Mr Croft
I learnt coding using Microsoft
Preparation for life was ultra-soft
In my school

Microsoft

I love the jab
When it's fast and sharp
That's hard
It's breaks all morale
Plus noses teeth and jaws
And there's more
Jab the body
Cause some pain
Insane
Cool the aggressor
Make them know better
And that you're a boxer
I love the jab

Jab

Ifie Porter
Two time national amateur champ
Knock out specialist
Out of the Brixton camp
He's put so many to sleep
After that first bell sings
His opponents commonly regret
As for days their heads ring
They didn't realise Minister Ifie
Is a devout dispatcher
Miguel's has already been blessed
By the great Body Snatcher
Surely God is good
Ifie Porter
Collecting future belts
Like he should

Ifie

3

ESOTERIC

In a sea
That never moved
Captured floating free
A song of silence
From afar
Sounds loud to comfort me
As stillness woke
Emotions calmed
The quietest bells began
Seen pictured mute
Her light absorbed
My painted angel sang

Stillness

It seemed so ridiculous
A sight rare and so obscure
Raging powers hidden by distance
In a land where beings are sure
Acidic clouds transformed into music
As debris built mansions
Far away
The fates were so creative
On that day

Debris

Closed my eyes
Suddenly words gush and flow
Seeing so many
A clarity that just grows
Gods and worlds
Heroes and smiles
Demons with fangs
Caravans stretched for miles
Words shining bright
Touch my head with a light
Fragrant pictures
That echo for years

Echo

I talked with a man
In a small silver room
Who knew things
That I couldn't see
He taught me about death
About love
Fortitude
And the angel
That travels
With me

Fortitude

I am here
Just as I am
Not for fate
I am what I am
I don't create life
I don't kill
I don't move
I exist without will
I don't degrade
Improve
Or stand still
Understand
Just as I am
I am here

Degrade

A river of pure silver flowed
Shimmering and vivid
It ran through mountains
As you laughed
And you danced
The day was dark and misty
I saw no life anywhere
Apart from you
So engaged
In a trance

Vivid

4

PHILOSOPHIC

Have you ever harpooned a tuna
Have you ever caught a fish
Do you have any idea
How it ended up
On your dish
Have you ever picked a pineapple
Or dug peanuts
From the ground
Does the food you eat hold no interest
Or is it a world profound

Tuna

Value your space
It's what nature gives
Take care of your space
It makes good thoughts live
Develop your space
Create the things of this world
Understand your space
Your being is sovereign girl
Value your space
Live in bliss
With nature kiss
Please love yourself

Develop

Beauty
Will save us all
Heal the sick
Lift those who fall
The flowers
Will remove all the stains
Let joy come and abide
Still the storms
Lower the tides
As the bloom
Be in love
Once again

Flowers

As a child I glared
Into a world
I didn't know
Held in her arms
A mother sees
Her future grow

Recognising shapes
I learned to navigate
Knowing love
In it's transience
And that people hate

Glared

I come from near the equator
So my hue is dark
That's what your skin says
When the Sun doest bark
All men are the same
Apart from travel and flight
Nature details the changes
In this persistence of light

Light

If time has no end
And mind has no bound
What limits you
What limits you
If space is so vast
And resources too
What limits you
What limits you

Limits

Beauty
With a breathtaking
Symmetry
Like
Those impossible puzzles
Revealing insights compelling
Rigid confinement
Declaring liberty in each dwelling
Each second made waste
So valuable so dear
Uniquely precious
Created once, and so rare
Like
Symmetry
With a breathtaking
Beauty

Symmetry

I was born alone
Me little me
In that dark womb
Not a soul did I see
No one's felt this pain
Tasted my bitter reality
Leave me be
I'll die by myself
Just noisy worms in my grave
Only I walked
That pathway
The one my will paved
Leave me be
Me little me
I was born alone

Grave

Insects like to bite
Anger likes a fight
Birds were born to fly
Each man will surely die
Cats will run up trees
Babies are rarely birthed in threes
Lightning strikes before it sounds
A woman's mind is sacred ground

Sacred

I'm in the backseat
Not in control
Exactly where I'm going
Nobody knows
I don't speak to the driver
He seems so busy
Here in the backseat
Happy me

Backseat

I don't believe
All my life
Never bought
The breeze
Or the rain
And the Sun
Is just fun
I don't believe

Bought

Some days you need a hammer
Some days you need a nail
Some days you need sunshine
And then rain to prevail
Some days you need laughter
Fun until you cry
Some days you need peace
Like a childhood
Lullaby

Hammer

Born in different ages
Die under the same Sun
Using many languages
But all have one tongue
Some stand on others
As on ground they all stand
Small are the degrees
That separate man

Separate

It's all so complex
I don't understand
Am I stupid
Or is this all planned
I'm really confused
None of this is clear
Could you simplify
Or get the hell
Out of here

Stupid

I don't dream your dreams
I don't walk in your shoes
I don't think your thoughts
Or see this world just like you
I can't imagine your journey
And what fate has put you through
But I'll listen
And be present
That's all I can do

Present

As the cat purred
It slowed it's breath
Contemplating
The peace of the moment
In static grace
With its frozen elegance
It closed its eyes
And began to dream

Cat

I was made for greatness
Made for nothing less
Excuse me if I want nothing less
For you
I was made for greatness
You can see it in my smile
Life is short
Be happy
Before you're through

Greatness